The Joys of Friendship

· *Believing in Ourselves* ·

The Joys of Friendship

A Book for Women

Arlene F. Benedict

Ariel Books

·

**Andrews McMeel
Publishing**

Kansas City

Contents

Introduction

Friendship is complex yet basic, simple yet profound. Calling upon our loyalty and dedication, friendship allows us to experience fully our ability to love others. With our friends, we trust, we share, we occasionally argue, and we always forgive. For our friends, we put our needs on the back burner, when we have to, and place theirs first; we know that we can count on them to return such kindness, but that is not why we do it. We do it because that is the way of love, and friendship is a form of love, a force that sustains, nurtures, helps us grow, and lets us be ourselves.

This book, then, is a gift for you and your friends. Collected here are quotations and essays that will help you recognize your potential to be a true friend to others, and to appreciate those who are true friends for you.

What Is Friendship?

*Friendship . . . helps us celebrate good times
and endure bad ones*

Life is full of highs and lows. Our happiness is magnified when our friends share it with us, and our sadness diminishes when our friends help us bear it. In good times we celebrate with our friends and partake in their joy. And during tough times, we reassure them that we will see them through their pain.

It is fun, certainly, (and easy) to share good times with our friends; when their fortunes change, however, it may be easier for us to shy away from them, but we must overcome this inclination—our friends deserve better.

Simply listening sympathetically when they tell us what they are going through can bolster our friends immeasurably. Sometimes all it takes is a voice—ours—to assure them that things will get better. Genuine friends are not scared off by hardships; staying by their side, we help them withstand life's trials and know that when we hit valleys in our own lives, our friends will be there to pull us to higher ground.

Today, I will both laugh and cry with my friends.

My friends are my estate.

—Emily Dickinson

Even though I can't solve your problems, I will be there
as your sounding board whenever you need me.

—Sandra K. Lamberson

Best friend, my wellspring in the wilderness!

—George Eliot

Are we not like the two volumes of one book?

—Marceline Desbordes-Valmore

There isn't much that I can do,
But I can sit an hour with you,
And I can share a joke with you,
And sometimes share reverses, too . . .
As on our way we go.

—Maude V. Preston

You are a thing of beauty and a joy forever.

—Louisa May Alcott
Little Women

The older I get the simpler my fantasies.
Two women sitting across a table from each other,
two cups of coffee, strong as the love.

—Pam Houston

Friendship is . . . a relationship based on the golden rule

Do unto others as you would have them do unto you. The language is old-fashioned but the principle is never out of fashion. It is the standard upon which all deep and long-lived friendships are based.

Employing the golden rule means little more than thinking about how we treat our friends and asking ourselves, "How would I like to be treated?" With our friends, we occasionally lay blame or jump to conclusions, but we also grant second chances and give them the benefit of the doubt. Instead of carrying grudges or feeling resentful, we try to be understanding and forgiving. Sometimes, our first response to our friends' success and accomplishments may be jealousy, but, rising above this emotion, we offer our sincere congratulations and good wishes.

Even when we have our own problems, we help our friends through theirs; taking turns, we boost each other's morale. After a spat, instead of sulking around with wounded pride, we make a real effort to reconcile. Friends listen as well as talk, give as well as receive, trust as well as accept trust, and forgive as well as accept forgiveness.

By practicing the golden rule we instill respect and kindness into our friendships, and build relationships that, though they may bend occasionally, will not break.

Today, I will treat my friends as I would have them treat me.

We are each other's reference point at our turning points.

—Elizabeth Fishel

There was a definite process by which one made
people into friends, and it involved talking to them
and listening to them for hours at a time.

—Rebecca West

It is prudent to pour the oil of delicate
politeness upon the machinery of friendship.

—Colette

What do we live for, if it is not to make
life less difficult for each other?

—George Eliot

What I expect from my male friends is that they are polite and clean.
What I expect from my female friends is unconditional love, the
ability to finish my sentences for me when I am sobbing, a complete
and total willingness to pour their hearts out to me . . .

—Anna Quindlen

Friendship is . . . a profound connection between two people

Most of us go through life with many acquaintances but only a few true friends. Even for those of us possessed of many friends, we always have several with whom we feel a special kind of affinity, a closeness somehow absent from our other relationships, however fulfilling they may be.

With these few true friends we can relax and let down our guard, revealing our dreams and plans for the future and our deepest hopes and aspirations, always knowing that our secrets are safe, and that we won't be ridiculed for our thoughts. These are the people to whom we confide our most burdensome worries and insecurities. Our real friends do not lie to us, even when telling a fib may be easier than telling the truth; instead, when talking about painful subjects, they look us in the eye. With true friends, we are truly honest.

Making allowances for each other's idiosyncrasies, we do not try to change or mold our friends; we love them not in spite of but because of their quirks. Accepted for who and what we are, we grant the same acceptance in return.

Today, I will celebrate the closeness of our friendship and the honesty we share.

Thought fitted thought; opinion met opinion:
we coincided, in short, perfectly.

—Charlotte Brontë
Jane Eyre

Sometimes, with luck, we find the kind of true
friend, male or female, that appears only two or three times
in a lucky lifetime, one that will winter us and summer
us, grieve, rejoice, and travel with us.

—Barbara Holland

I have learned that to have a good friend
is the purest of all God's gifts, for it is a love that
has no exchange of payment.

—Frances Farmer

Yes'm, old friends is always best, 'less you can
catch a new one that's fit to make an old one out of.

—Sarah Orne Jewett

You said just the thing that I wished you to say.
And you made me believe that you meant it.

—Grace Stricker Dawson

Intimacies between women often go
backwards, beginning in revelations and ending
in small talk without loss of esteem.

—Elizabeth Bowen

Friendship is . . . a living entity that we must nurture

Like a pear tree, friendship will bear fruit only if it is well cared for; in order to weather the changes wrought by the seasons of our lives, it must be nurtured and protected.

More than just shelter it, we must actively encourage our friendship to flourish. For a relationship to span years (decades even), it has to grow; if we mature but our relationship does not, it can become confining, and we may find ourselves wondering why we no longer feel at home inside it. Perhaps our relationship has become routine: we always do the same things, talk about the same topics. Boredom might be our response, and we might be tempted to abandon the friendship. But just because the relationship is in a rut does not mean we should forsake it; on the contrary, we should work to revitalize it. Perhaps we can share a new hobby together, or go somewhere that we've never been before. Chances are that new experiences like these will rejuvenate our flagging friendship.

If we are devoted, we are willing and able to evolve together; to do nothing is to risk stifling the friendship. How much better to nurture our friendship so that it grows with us, ripening and deepening, with the passing years.

Today, I will work to keep my friendships healthy and alive.

The true test of friendship is to be able to sit
or walk with a friend for an hour in perfect silence
without wearying of one another's company.

—Dinah Maria Mulock Craik

•

The growth of true friendship may be a lifelong affair.

—Sarah Orne Jewett

•

No person is your friend who demands your silence,
or denies your right to grow.

—Alice Walker

Hold a true friend with both your hands.

—African proverb

Each friend represents a world in us, a world
possibly not born until they arrive, and it is only by this
meeting that a new world is born.

—Anaïs Nin

That is the best—to laugh with someone
because you both think the same things are funny.

—Gloria Vanderbilt

Friendship . . . is created by small gestures, not grand ones

With little gestures that express our affection, friendship grows. Just as life, for the most part, is lived one day at a time, so friendship is created step by step by step.

We brighten our friends' days by sending birthday cards and flowers to their office. When our friends are sick with the flu, we bring them chicken soup and make them tea. And when they are experiencing tensions at home or at work, our supportive phone calls can lessen their stress. Understanding what our friends are going through, and offering just the right dose of compassion, encouragement, or gaiety at just the right moment, is the way of friendship.

A solid friendship is like a well-built house: The foundation must be strong in order for the edifice to be stable. Through care and thoughtfulness, we construct this steady foundation. It may seem a daunting process, but as with building a house, friendship is really erected brick by brick, resulting in a fortress that can withstand anything.

Today, I will find time to do at least one act of kindness for a friend.

There is something irreducibly mysterious
about the genesis of friendships.

—Christine Leefeldt

•

We should not let the grass grow on the path of friendship.

—Marie Thérèse Rodet Geoffrin

•

Do not keep the alabaster boxes of your love and tenderness
sealed up until your friends are dead. Fill their lives with sweetness.
Speak approving and cheering words while their ears can hear
them and while their hearts can be thrilled by them.

—Henry Ward Beecher

"Stay" is a charming word in a friend's vocabulary.

—Louisa May Alcott

We have been talking as old friends should talk,
about nothing, about everything.

—Lillian Hellman

It is the friends you can call up at 4 A.M. that matter.

—Marlene Dietrich

Friendship . . . must be mended quickly after conflicts

Pride, anger, and impatience can sometimes assail even the strongest friendships. When they do, feelings get hurt, and we may be tempted to retreat from our friend because it is easier than working out our differences. The more quickly we soothe our strained emotions, however, the faster we confirm our commitment to the friendship.

Sometimes we feel so free to express ourselves with our friends that, before we realize it, we say things we don't really mean, causing harsh words to erupt and tempers to flare. When this happens, we should try to resolve things quickly, with love and compassion and not with force or coercion, which only engender resentment.

To patch up our differences, we must seek the common ground, finding points on which to agree, and genuinely trying to see each other's position. On some issues, of course, we will just have to agree to disagree. What is crucial, however, is that we reestablish the bond of friendship immediately.

Made not of concrete but of volatile human feelings, friendships need to be handled with care, particularly if they are bruised. Those that are repaired quickly will survive conflicts big and small and be even more resilient because of them.

Today, I will forgive quickly.

You can always tell a real friend:
When you've made a fool of yourself he doesn't
feel you've done a permanent job.

—Laurence J. Peter

·

The problems that plague a friendship are rarely
one hundred percent the other person's fault.
We should self-examine carefully before we make
up our mind—and before we close it.

—Judith Viorst

A friend is a present you give yourself.

—Robert Louis Stevenson

A friend may well be reckoned
with a masterpiece of nature.

—George Eliot

What I cannot love, I overlook.
Is that real friendship?

—Anäis Nin

True friendship is never serene.

—Marie de Sévigné

Friendship . . . builds up our self-esteem and self-confidence

For our occasional bouts of self-doubt or sagging self-esteem there is a sure remedy: our friends. During these times, our friends assure us that, yes, we will get the job we applied for, or that we still look great even though we have gained a few pounds.

When we can see nothing in ourselves but our weaknesses, our friends will point out our strengths; when we worry about our failings, our friends enumerate our successes. Knowing that our friends think we are trustworthy, lovable, and capable makes it easier for us to believe in ourselves. The effect of our boosted self-esteem is far-reaching: We have the confidence to take on new endeavors and set our sights on lofty goals.

And so, even when the world outside our friendship bruises our egos, inside our friendship our confidence builds and self-esteem rises.

Today, I will give support and encouragement to my friends and accept happily the support they give to me.

For all of us, by permitting us to see ourselves in the mirror of their affection, friends help to anchor our self-image, to validate our identity.

—Lillian B. Rubin

Female friendships that work are relationships in which women help each other to belong to themselves.

—Louise Bernikow

Woman softens her own troubles by
generously solacing those of others.

—Françoise D'Aubegne Maintenon

If we would build on a sure foundation in friendship,
we must love our friends for their sakes than for our own.

—Charlotte Brontë

The language of friendship is not words but meanings.

—Henry David Thoreau

If, after I go out, a friend of mine gave a feast, and did not invite me to it, I shouldn't mind a bit. I can be perfectly happy by myself. . . . But if, after I go out, a friend of mine had a sorrow, and refused to allow me to share it, I should feel it most bitterly. If he shut the doors of the house of mourning against me I would come back again and again and beg to be admitted, so that I might share in what I was entitled to share in. If he thought me unworthy, unfit to weep with him, I should feel it as the most poignant humiliation, as the most terrible mode in which disgrace could be inflicted on me.

—Oscar Wilde

Friendship . . . is built upon trust

There can be no friendship without trust as its foundation. When meeting new people—potential friends—we are cautious about what we reveal to them, letting down our guard slowly. It is a screening process, one that can take days or months, in order to assure us that these new people are trustworthy: They won't steal our thunder or scoff at our aspirations and beliefs.

The metamorphosis from acquaintance to friend is difficult to trace, but at some point, a colleague, neighbor, or schoolmate turns into a friend. Unconsciously, we have placed our trust in them and they, too, have placed theirs in us. Trust is critical not only for forming friendships, but for sustaining them. As we become closer friends, our trust grows and so does our willingness to confide in each other.

Although trust is an unspoken promise never to betray each other, we occasionally do break this promise—usually inadvertently. If this happens, trust must be reestablished if the friendship is to be salvaged. Rebuilding trust is never easy, but losing a beloved friend is much, much harder.

Today, I will honor the trust that exists in my friendships.

Oh, the comfort, the inexpressible comfort of feeling safe with a person, having neither to weigh thoughts nor measure words, but pouring them all right out, just as they are, chaff and grain together; certain that a faithful hand will take and sift them, keep what is worth keeping, and then with the breath of kindness throw the rest away.

—Dinah Maria Mulock Craik

I always felt that the great high privilege, relief, and comfort of friendship was that one had to explain nothing.

—Katherine Mansfield

A friend can tell you things you don't want to tell yourself.

—Frances Ward Wheeler

It takes a lot of courage to show your dreams to someone else.

—Erma Bombeck

•

I can trust my friends. . . .
These people force me to examine myself,
encourage me to grow.

—Cher

•

A friend is a person with whom you dare to be yourself.

—Frank Crane

Special Friends

Friends are . . . our brothers and sisters

Who can't remember a family car ride when our parents threatened to turn the car around because we were fighting with our brothers and sisters in the backseat? Even if we were extremely close and affectionate with our siblings while growing up, there were always times when we wanted nothing to do with them.

Regardless of our relationship as children, our brothers and sisters can be fantastic friends to us. Perhaps, we have gone our separate ways for years, and then one day we begin to reacquaint ourselves. Getting to know each other as adults can be a wonderful experience.

With our friends, no matter how close, we tend to be somewhat on guard; not so with our brothers and sisters. Because they grew up alongside us, our brothers and sisters have a unique and unequaled insight into our character and personality. We can openly and bluntly express ourselves to them, no beating around the bush; if something is bothering us, our brothers and sisters often pick up on it long before anyone else. This sensitivity allows soul searching talks to occur naturally, and often.

How lucky we are to count our brothers and sisters among our friends, not just our relatives.

Today, I will celebrate the special bond I share with my sister or brother.

In thee my soul shall own combined
The sister and the friend.

—Catherine Killigrew

Our siblings. They resemble us just enough
to make all their differences confusing, and no
matter what we choose to make of this, we are cast
in relation to them our whole lives long.

—Susan Scarf Merrell

It is one of the blessings of old friends
that you can afford to be stupid with them.

—Ralph Waldo Emerson

A friend is one who knows all
about you and likes you anyway.

—Christi Mary Warner

Sisters stand between one and life's cruel circumstances.

—Nancy Mitford

•

The relationship between two siblings
is perhaps more like a cactus than an oak,
for it requires less watering than other
friendships in order to survive.

—Susan Scarf Merrell

Friends are . . . our husbands and wives

One of the deepest devotions we can know is the love shared between husbands and wives. Such dedication goes beyond friendship; we are lovers, parents, lifelong partners, trusted advisers, joyful cocreators of the future.

All of the best advice about nurturing a friendship is doubly important here. With marriage come burdens that most friendships do not have to bear—finances, raising children, the effects of daily routine. It is, therefore, especially important to bring lightness and laughter into the relationship. Most important, we must never let our problems get in the way of our friendship because long after the children are grown up and the mortgage is paid off, we'll still be there for each other.

With marriage also come opportunities for closeness that most friendships do not offer: planning our future, helping each other to realize our dreams, making our mark in the world together. And though we continue to celebrate the qualities in each other that drew us together, we also encourage our spouse to grow and change.

This incredible friendship serves as a daily reminder of how much we are loved and how much we are capable of loving. In each other we see the passion we have for our lives, and we honor each other's need to be separate yet inseparable.

Today, I will bring joy and commitment to the special friendship I share with my spouse.

I would be friends with you and have your love.

—William Shakespeare

·

What greater thing is there for two human souls
than to feel that they are joined . . . to strengthen
each other . . . to be at one with each
other in silent unspeakable memories.

—George Eliot

Two people holding each other up like flying buttresses.
Two people depending on each other and babying each other
and defending each other against the world outside.

—Erica Jong

Friendship is to feel as one while remaining two.

—Madame Schwetchine

I have found out that friendship is quite as important
as love and it isn't any easier than love.

—Brigitte Bardot

A beloved friend does not fill one part
of the soul, but penetrating the whole,
becomes connected with all feeling.

—William Ellery Channing

I breathed a song into the air,
It fell to earth, I knew not where. . . .
And the song, from beginning to end,
I found again in the heart of a friend.

—Henry Wadsworth Longfellow

Make a friend when you don't need one.

—Jamaican proverb

I keep my friends as misers do their treasure,
because, of all the things granted us by wisdom,
none is greater or better than friendship.

—Pietro Aretino

Friendship is love refined.

—Susannah Centlivre

Two may talk together under the same roof
for many years, yet never really meet; and two
others at first speech are old friends.

—Mary Catherwood

My best friend is the one who brings out the best in me.

—Henry Ford

Friendship is the sweetest form of love.

—Annie Gottlieb

The human heart, at whatever age,
opens only to the heart that opens in return.

—Maria Edgeworth

You might disagree about a political issue, or one of you will be a vegetarian and the other won't, but basically you share the same attitude toward life. You're tuned into the same wavelength, and until the circuit blows a fuse (as it might through life's circumstances), you follow the electricity of each other's thoughts.

—Adelaide Bry

In my friend, I find a second self.

—Isabel Norton

The text of this book
was set in Bembo and Isadora
by Sally McElwain.